LEADER LIFESTYLEZ VOL. 3

D.A.P. Your Way to Greatness:

Essentials for Success

ISBN: 9781723852039

CONTENTS

DREAMS

ACTIONS

POWER

WHAT SEPARATES A LEADER FROM A GREAT LEADER?

Does a title make a leader? Can a janitor or a waiter be a leader? Sure! Then what separates a great leader from a good leader?

There are many leaders, but only a select few are deemed good or great. Leaders are respected, but great leaders are remembered, becoming an undying inspiration and model to the many aspirants of each new generation.

A leader inspires people to have confidence in them, but a great leader inspires people to have confidence in themselves.

Leaders have the ability to delegate, the capacity to solve problems, and the power to manage others. Great leaders use learning, teaching, and personal drive to empower the people around them.

While a leader may be able to inspire and motivate their team members to accomplish tasks, a great leader does so with a sense of urgency. To be able to motivate others to action, you need to be able to communicate urgency to your team.

It can be difficult to pin down one specific thing; however, one major identifying trait of a great leader is that people always want to be around them.

One of the things a great leader does is lead by example. The leader will exemplify the behavior they want within their environment or business. A great leader understands that what needs to be done is just as important as who is going to do it. So they will appoint or recruit the best people available. Leaders will get many average people on their team to do what they direct them to do. The great leaders are not afraid to confront the brutal facts head on.

Good leaders are extremely disciplined. Good leaders will use their entire team in the decision-making process. Good leaders are very humble. When things are going well, the good leaders will give credit to everybody but themselves. If there is no one else to give credit to they will say they were fortunate. When things don't go well, they will take a good look in the mirror and take all the blame. A not so good leader may take credit and be able to tell you who is to blame when things go wrong.

A true leader always sets up the organization for success long after they are gone. Average leaders may be caught up with their own ego and would almost wish the company to fail just to show how indispensable they are. The great leaders are extremely determined. They infect the people around them with their drive for continuous sustained results. They have resolved to do everything they have to do to make the organization successful.

Leaders deliver output as expected. Great leaders surpass expectations, those otherwise thought as impossible. In the course of your leadership, many obstacles will come your way. While most will find ways to go around these obstacles, a great leader will seek opportunities from them. It's a natural instinct to stay in your comfort zone, but great leaders go out of them, seek out problems, and layout solutions to prevent them from happening. They believe in the power of anticipation, that the prevention is always better than the cure.

Do you need a prestigious label to be in charge? There are a number of great leaders around us that have yet to be discovered. There is a leader in each of us. Unfortunately, a lot of potentially great leaders are led by average leaders and learn incorrect styles of leadership that could prevent them from becoming great leaders. You have the potential to be a great leader. Read on to find out how you can become a great leader and mentor. Become the best leader you can be. Sure! You will be empowered to take action...achieving your dreams is certain.

DEFINITION OF A LEADER

What defines an effective leader? In order to determine what an effective leader is, you have to look at exactly what a leader's role is to begin with. A leader:

- ➢ Is willing to pay their dues.
- ➢ Knows how to lead.
- ➢ Cultivates an environment where each team member can develop to reach their fullest potential.
- ➢ Guides and points to resources.
- ➢ Identifies and develops future leaders which will duplicate their own level of effort and action.

In Order to Lead People You Must First Know How to Lead Yourself.

- ➢ Do you accomplish your goals?
- ➢ Do you have thick skin?

Leaders make it happen.

They visualize their own success and understand that in order to get the lifestyle they want, they have to "make it happen." In order to make it happen, they create goals and objectives within each goal that they know will move them forward to accomplish their goal; one goal at a time, each goal leading to the finish line.

A Leader NEVER caves to a challenge.

Leaders have this uncanny knack of finding solutions. They believe, know and understand that for every problem there is a solution. Because they know that challenges will arise, they readily deal with them rather than procrastinate, as some leaders may do with issues. It's all about developing the skills of getting to the solution and not focusing on the challenge. A leader will evaluate and deal with a challenge in the following manner:

- ➢ Identify the problem.
- ➢ Resolve the problem by creating a solution.

A Leader Cultivates an Environment.

Leaders understand the many facets that are involved with developing their people. They know how to utilize individual approaches which are specifically suited to every person, cultivating an environment where each person can openly participate and be "part of the family." A good leader breeds trust into their organization. When people are in a trusting environment, the sky is the limit.

Leaders Set the Pace.

Good leaders are excellent at evaluating the skill level of the individuals on their team and establishing a pace for them individually, according to the skill set they come to the table with (whether they are a newbie or a seasoned leader that they themselves work within a team setting.)

Leaders Guide and Point to Resources.

A good leader is a good pointer. Have you ever been at a crossroad and seen the signs pointing in every direction? Leaders are the sign-posts. They direct people to the resources and information that can help them develop to the next skill level.

Leaders Identify and Develop Future Leaders.

A good leader is always looking within their organization for those willing to take action and are serious about what they are doing. Good leaders produce good leaders because they know how to develop people. Good leaders attract and develop high quality people. They pass the baton to them and step out of the way, to allow them to learn how to become leaders under their mentorship.

THE AUTHENTIC LEADER LIFESTYLE

Many people think they cannot be great leaders. They believe that effective leaders must be people with extraordinary ability. If that is the way you think, you'd better change your mindset. Many people can be great leaders if they are authentic to themselves and others.

"All of us have the spark of leadership in us, whether in business, in government, or as a non-profit volunteer. The challenge is to understand ourselves enough to discover where we can use our leadership gifts to serve others. We are here for something. Life is about giving and living fully." - Ann Fudge.

Acknowledge that you can be a successful leader. As an authentic leader, you have an authentic lifestyle. The following ten points are attributes of this lifestyle.

1.   Your leadership is based on your life story

Everyone has a signature story to tell. Whether you went through some struggle during your childhood, faced challenges during your teenage years, or experienced hardship and difficult relationships during your adulthood, you were being prepared to lead at some point in your life.

Even if you think you did not go through a struggle and you were always blessed with the good things in life, you still have a story to tell. The story is about your life and the way you see the world and how you interacted with those who were suffering. When you build your leadership based on your signature story you inspire many and your influence will increase.

2. You are true to yourself and others

As an authentic leader you are true to yourself and others. You are honest and do not play political games. When you follow the truth, you do not need to hide anything. You do not need to imitate others and you do not need the approval of others. You are just yourself and that is what matters the most.

3. Your family is on top of your priority list

Authentic leaders who follow their own heart, your family has a special place in your life. You care about your spouse, parents, kids, and friends. You consult them for your decisions and find peace and strength by referring to them. You may choose your family over your career just because of your unconditional love for them, yet you know that you made the right decision because of your authenticity. You know that long-lasting success comes from within.

4. You have integrity

Integrity is the key in an authentic leaders' lifestyle. Without integrity, a leader cannot be authentic. Integrity has three aspects as follows:

a) You do not leave the tasks that you have started unfinished. You complete the incomplete and move forward.

b) Your thoughts, words, and deeds are one and the same. In other words, what you think is what you say and what you say is what you do.

c) You are the same person at home and at work. You are the same human being wherever you go and in whatever you do.

5. You live on purpose and lead on purpose

As an authentic leader you know your life's purpose and you choose actions to fulfill your purpose. You live on purpose and lead on purpose. You blend your personal and professional vision so that you have the best in mind for everyone in every situation. By living and leading on purpose, you live a happy and fulfilled life and leave a legacy for future generations.

6.   You lead without title

In 1991, I went on active duty and joined the United States Army. I started my military career as an enlisted soldier. I was a private, which was the lowest rank in the military. A few years after that, I became a Non-Commissioned Officer (NCO), and later, I became a Commissioned Officer (CO), a leader of enlisted soldiers and officers. During those years, I realized that all positions and titles are just labels. I noticed that those who cared more about their labels than the people would not be remembered by people when they eventually lose their labels. In contrast, those who cared more about people than labels, and respect people for who they are, and recognize them for what they do, will be respected, trusted, and remembered by people all the time.

Authentic leaders do not need titles to lead. You can be an employee without a title and lead authentically. When you do your best in everything you do and serve without any expectations in return, you are a leader with no title. Authentic leaders do not care about titles because they know that titles are temporary. They know that when they don't chase titles, titles will chase them instead and they will get great rewards in return.

7. You are a visionary

As an authentic leader, you are a visionary. You have a vision for your organization and you are able to paint your vision clearly. As an authentic leader, you grant vision to others. You help them see what they could not see otherwise. You inspire them to become visionary and authentic in the same way that you are.

8. You believe in yourself and others

Authentic leaders have full trust in themselves and others. As an authentic leader, you know that the circle of trust starts with you. When you trust others first, you become worthy of trust in their mind. You believe in your own capabilities and those of the people around you. As a result, you give them confidence to be creative and try new things without fear of failure. The result will be long-lasting success.

9. You know the value of working with people

As an authentic leader, you know that working with people is the secret to your success. If you work with people and for people, they will do wonders for you, especially in tough times. John C. Maxwell said, "Leaders must be close enough to relate to others, but far enough

15

ahead to motivate them." As an authentic leader, you expand the circle of your friends and network by becoming close to people. Expanding your network is the key to expanding your net worth.

10. You don't need external motivators to lead

Authentic leadership comes from within. You lead with your heart and soul. You lead with love, passion, and energy. You do not need external motivators to lead because you are inspired to do your best and inspire others to do their best as well. When you live and lead on purpose, you have the fire within yourself that burns all the time and drives the wheel of your passion and motivation.

ARE YOU A GOOD LEADER OR A GREAT LEADER?

Throughout history, there have been great leaders of industry who have revolutionized our lives, leaders of military forces who have won famous battles and leaders of countries who have changed entire societies.

Likewise, not-so-great leaders permeate our history and can unfortunately have a far more lasting effect on our lives than the great ones. Poor leaders have caused the collapse of companies and institutions, caused atrocities in the name of freedom and created hardship for millions of their people.

In business, as in all walks of life, there are people who really shouldn't be leaders. They may have inherited their position, or been in the right place at the right time, or perhaps just knew the right people.

Of course a leader needs to be confident, be able to communicate, manage a team of people and be able to make important decisions. But what separates an average leader from a good or great leader?

Celebrities

Historically, people sought guidance and inspiration from religious leaders, political leaders and even "celebrities". In recent times and for those above certain age and intelligence, the honor has passed from the likes of David Beckham and winners of Big Brother to business leaders such as Richard Branson, and Alan Sugar. Business leaders are the new celebrities and have become some of the most influential members of society.

Good business leaders have a responsibility to their shareholders and focus on the vision and strategies of their company to grow market share and increase revenue and profit. Great business leaders also assign focus and effort into another part of their company. They understand that getting this part right will have a dramatic positive effect on the success of their business. They also focus on their people.

Ordinary People

Most people have a job, working for an employer for a third of their day, most days of the week. Work is a huge part of our lives and should be an enjoyable, positive experience. "The way we make a living, the jobs we have, and the way our work is rewarded have tremendous bearing on our lives, making them exciting and rewarding, or dull and anxious." (Good Business, Mihaly Csikszentmihalyi)

Whether CEOs of thousands or managers of a few, business leaders need to recognize the responsibility they have for the wellbeing of their people. Strong leaders know that their company's most important asset is its people. They know the importance of sharing their vision and goals, not just with their customers and the press, but also with their teams. They make sure that their messages reach all of their people at all levels of the company.

Great leaders are great listeners; they listen to their clients, their peers and their people. They foster an environment where every person in the company can have a say, has the opportunity to present an idea, to be taken seriously and made to feel that they are an important part of the company or team.

So, if you're an OK leader, can you be a good leader? If you're a good leader, can you be a great one? And if you're not currently a leader or manager, could you become one? Do you possess the inherent qualities beyond the usual business skills needed to meet commercial targets?

At all stages of our careers, we should strive to improve, to learn, to question the way things are done and to explore the potential to improve. The best leaders will have the strength to admit that they don't know everything. Ask your customers and your people what they want; too many leaders simply decide for them.

In these current difficult times, where companies all over are reducing their workforce, it's critically important that the skills of those remaining are invested in and improved upon. In good or bad times, growing your internal talent will increase the loyalty and commitment of your people and give you a competitive advantage.

"Employers who retain their staff and develop their workforce are best placed to respond to economic recovery because they have the talent to innovate and the expertise to maintain successful customer relationships. In fact, employers that don't invest in training are two-and-a-half times more likely to fail. (Training and Establishment Survival - Sector Skills Development Agency March 2007).

Passionate Leadership

Passionate Leadership - Creating an environment of purpose and passion in the workplace.

Great leaders create a company that rises far beyond the goals of the bottom line. Great leaders strive to hit a higher target in the way they maximize every employee by finding ways to leverage the passion of each employee in order to create incentives that go well beyond financial rewards. Sure people work because they need a paycheck, but they stay and give their all because their work has deeper meaning than the check they get. Great leaders get this.

The greatest leaders rely on a simple, timeless idea in order to create passionate, purposeful organizations: the highest purpose in life is growth. We're not talking about the current popular notions of growth here -- e.g. growth of your bank account, mortgage payment, or waistline. No, this notion of personal growth goes back to the ancient Greeks: growth in wisdom, in maturity and in one's contribution to society.

So how do we go about creating an environment where people thrive and personal growth is pursued? Leadership must determine the organization's purpose. What is the real mission of the company or organization? Why is it in existence? In healthcare, we have the unique opportunity to meet the needs of patients in a very physical, emotional and spiritual way. Morrow and Cavasin stated, "The purpose of an organization must go beyond financial concerns and speak to the ancient, growth-inspiring question of contribution to society. Some of the oldest, most successful companies in the world -- e.g. Johnson & Johnson (founded 1886), GE (1892), Citicorp (1812) -- owe their success to the relentless pursuit of a single, society-impacting purpose."

After you determine your reason for existence, the next step must be to create incentives for your employees that motivate them and their passions. How? You can't impose passion on a person; however, you can create an environment where the mission, vision and values of your company are fully embraced by the employees. Employees should be offered numerous opportunities to discover how their individual roles support the overall mission. This can be done in a number of ways.

Passionate Organizations have environments with the following attributes:

The mission, vision and values of the company are clearly communicated. The organizational purpose is known and embraced. All of your leaders must communicate the corporate purpose clearly. They must exhibit their own personal commitment to the purpose. If one of your leaders doesn't embrace your organization's overall organizational purpose and culture, you may have to let them go. They will do more harm to your company than the good they bring in their individual role – guaranteed! Great leaders interact directly with small groups of employees until they "get it;" to screen new employees for cultural fit; and to constantly keep the relevance of purpose and passion clear for everyone.

Reward passion and excellence - add this component into performance reviews. Celebrate individual and group success as a company/organization. Give back to the community as a collective group. Promote blood drives. Help families in need. Show your employees through your corporate actions that you care.

Trust - Make sure you hire aggressive over-achievers that buy into your organizations purpose and mission and then let them run. Most employees empowered with independence and responsibility will rise to the occasion. Those that don't will typically opt out and move to a company where they feel more comfortable (Win-win for both sides).

Leadership by example - Leaders must be passionate, mature, self-aware, and self-confident. They must promote passion, purpose, and growth to the same degree they promote financial objectives. They must not be threatened by the passions and aspirations of others, but instead they must have the integrity to resolve disagreements or power struggles through communication rather than confrontation.

Clearly, leadership is different from management. Don't enlist professional managers. What you want are professional leaders and you will see your organization reach heights you have never seen before.

THE MOTIVATIONAL LEADER

The term motivation is from the Greek word, "Kino", meaning to "move" or "propel". It is a powerful force that can move any individual from zero to hero. Its effect can be so contagious that someone who once thought it was impossible to make it in life suddenly realizes that "I can do it" when hearing a motivating word from someone who was once a failure but later became successful. That is the power of motivation. Newton's first law of motion says, "Every object assumes a state of rest until an external force is applied to it." That external force can be likened to "motivation" while we are the "object" in question.

We all need motivation to begin, and to begin is to win. As Jim Ryun puts it, "motivation is what gets you started; habit is what keeps you going." You can never form the habit of doing anything which you are not motivated to do in the first place. So motivation is the ignition key that awakens the engine in you. Once that engine starts running, it never stops except by your permission.

The great challenge is that a lot of us find it difficult to get started. We can be so comfortable in our comfort zones; not willing to take risks. T.S. Elliot said, "Only those who risk going too far can possibly find out how far they can go." You never know what you can do until you try. As Zig Ziglar said, "The secret of getting ahead is getting started". Life is a daring adventure and it takes daring people who are internally motivated to move out and achieve great success.

A motivational leader is someone who is internally motivated not only to motivate himself, but takes it as a responsibility to motivate others. As a manager, supervisor, and CEO of an organization, you are a motivational leader and your employee's motivation should be your utmost concern and responsibility.

As a motivational leader, your starting point to motivational leadership is to begin seeing yourself as a role model, seeing yourself as an example to others. See yourself as a person who sets the standard that others follow. Many business managers, entrepreneurs, and CEOs are not aware of the effects that motivation can have on their business, and it is therefore important they learn and understand the factors that determine positive motivation in the workplace. Lee Iacocca said, "Motivation is everything. You can do the work of two people, but you can't be two people. Instead, you have to inspire the next guy down the line and get him to inspire his people". Therefore, as a leader, you should understand that the influence you have on your subordinates help boost their morale into giving their best at work.

A healthy leader motivates rather than demotivates. They always seek to focus on achieving their organization's primary mission by raising the energy and momentum of their followers to work towards achieving the same goal. The question is: what are those qualities that motivational leaders possess that enables them to increase the energy of their people in boosting productivity at work? Let us examine a few such qualities:

They know the personality of their team: As Henry Ford, Founder of Ford Motors once said, "Coming together is a beginning. Keeping together is progress. Working together is success." Motivational leaders are really amazing in the sense that they understand the personality of their team members that helps "keep together" as a team in achieving sustainable progress. Research has shown that people respond well to recognition, rewards and incentives. The majority of them value relationships and respond to an open, social atmosphere to be able to work well. As a motivational leader, you are the initiator and your people look up to you to nurture the atmosphere of good working relationships.

Set the Example: Motivational leaders recognize that their positive lifestyle is a source of motivation to those they are leading. For this reason, they strive to set an exemplary lifestyle that others emulate. They know that their actions are closely examined by those they lead and one wrong signal from them could lead to the loss of their credibility.

Communicate vision for the future: It has been said that vision is the crystal clear mental picture of a desirable future you hope to see. In other words, your vision is your future. As a motivational leader, your followers will follow you to the degree you guide them to the desirable future. No one wants to follow a blind leader who cannot see beyond their environment. And followers can sense when a leader is incapable of leading them. They begin to feel the uneasiness of being in one spot with no future in view.

Empower others to lead: As a motivational leader, your commitment to developing leaders will ensure ongoing growth to the organization and to people. Realizing that people are your most valuable asset, and that providing the opportunity for their growth to becoming effective leaders is not an option but a necessity that should be a top priority on your agenda as a motivational leader.

Look beyond the followers' weaknesses: Throughout life, we acquire abilities and skills that help us to reach our goals and fulfill our purpose in life. We also have under developed areas or weaknesses that need improvement. A motivational leader may choose not to reprimand followers when they fall short in their ability, but rather, encourage them and help them in their areas of weaknesses. As leaders, it is our job to help position them to play to their strengths. This would do wonders for their confidence, thereby preparing them for greater success.

Reward and Appreciate Accomplishments: The motivational leaders understand that to keep others motivated, they need to be appreciated and rewarded for good effort and for tasks performed – well. Things like thank you "John" for carrying the assignment well or sending a short message through email or better still, posting on a bulletin board the outstanding employee of the month, is highly recommended to push the employees' productivity.

Peak Performance Leadership & Business Development Expert - Elvis Ukpaka - provides impact-FULL Leadership, Self-Improvement and Business Development training and coaching solutions to high profile individuals and organizations. His reputation for helping people achieve peak performance at work, and in life, derives from a burning passion to deliver unparalleled value, by empowering his audience to actualize their potentials to become successful leaders and high performers.

DREAMS

WHAT IS YOUR DREAM?

A dream is the wish to have or be something, especially one that seems difficult to achieve. It is the vision and aspiration someone has in life. In other words, dream and vision can be used interchangeably. Without vision, one does not and cannot go far in life: and anyone of such is not fit for existence, he is not fit to live. Its importance can not be overemphasized in today's life. Many people just wander about in life without a definite destination. They circle around in the dark while missing the pathway to the light. Tragic enough, most people never trace their steps back to the right path, because if one does not know where he is going, he should at least know where he is coming from. Knowing your source is paramount in retracing destiny.

"This dream which I have dreamed!" Joseph said (Genesis 37:6 KJV). This is the starting point in the journey of life and destiny. Without a dream, you will live a dreary life; a life with no clear direction. Having a definite vision for life is pertinent as it determines your destiny and future as well as your personality. Joseph had a dream that he was destined to become a great man. His dream was a positive one, not a negative vision of someone chasing him with a cutlass trying to harm him. Rather, he had a tangible vision that would propel him to kingship. "...my sheaf arose, and also stood upright; and behold, your sheaves stood round about, and made obeisance to my sheaf." This is worth associating with. Joseph's vision was to become a king, a leader of his brethren as well as his generation. It is not a servitudinal one; rather, it is a vision that would later create a non-existing position of a prime minister of the great nation of his time. The point here is that it all started in a dream. That is what determines who you would be in life.

What is your dream? What is your reason for existence? Why were you born? The answers to these questions are necessary in determining your personality as well as who you will become in life. Joseph had a vision and it catapulted him to Egyptian Prime Minister. Your vision will take you to the enviable height you desire. Without aiming at a target, you most likely will never hit it. Your dream is what you see and have imagined that you can get and possess. Desire is the output of dream. When you dream of anything, you desire it and what you desire with determination backed with faith, you can achieve. Though Joseph's brothers stood against him in becoming great, he never quit; and finally his vision took him to a position that may have ordinarily seemed impossible. Dreams remove impossibilities from a man's life; with dreams all things are possible. Therefore, having a vision in life is the bedrock of success. "I HAVE DREAMED!" Joseph said. A very good one; the type that can lead to greatness, fulfillment, establishment, prosperity, kingship, as well as higher ground. It is so great that analyzing it may take several books and great effort and thought. Joseph had a dream, what is your dream?

What surprised me mostly and I really learned from it, is Joseph's second dream. Though Joseph's dream was such a great one, that was not the end of it. He had another one, greater than the first dream. Hear him, "Look, I have dreamed another dream." And this time, the sun, the moon, and the eleven stars bowed down to me" (Genesis 37:9 NKJV). Whoa! This is wonderful! Though Joseph's first dream was fantastic, there was still more to the story. "In his second dream, there was not only eleven sheaves, not only eleven stars, but also the moon and the sun" that bowed to him." His first vision was that of greatness, but there was more to that. Joseph wanted the best for himself and his people. He wanted to achieve his fullest potential. He never lost faith in his dreams. He could see beyond ordinary leadership even when he led just few. He made the best out of life. Settling for just the good could have jeopardized his divine purpose; and that could have been disastrous. This is the type of dream that sets the atmosphere for success. For one to become great he must have extra-ordinary vision, the type that knows neither barriers nor limitations. Joseph told his brothers that he had another dream, but not like the normal story they already knew about. It was not a usual vision but an unusual one that would make him an extraordinary leader. "But this time..." not the previous time, not last year's dream but now.

What is your dream now? What have you dreamed about before and what are you dreaming about now? Joseph had a wonderful dream but that did not stop him from dreaming again for greater. Dreamers are leaders. If you can't dream, you may never reach your purpose or potential. Vision in life takes you to places of honour. Without vision, you could lead an unfulfilling life of mediocrity. You become useless in meaningful endeavours if you never realize your purpose and walk in it. The ability for you to dream and renew it progressively can make you an icon and legend in the world. It is tragic if one dies without a dream, but even more tragic is the man that dies without ever making the effort to realize his dreams. When you have a vision, the next thing is to work towards its actualization, taking into consideration that there are dream killers out there. Now look at what Joseph's brothers said when he was bringing them food.

...behold, this dreamer cometh. "Come now therefore, and let us slay him, and cast him into some pit... and we shall see what will become of his dreams" (Genesis 37:19-20 KJV). Joseph wanted his brothers' comfort. He cared for and loved them, but they did not want his plans and visions to come through. They hated him and his visions and planned on killing him despite his good heart towards them. There are people like that in the world today. People do not want you to have a vision higher than theirs. They hate you when your aspirations are great, and they may see you as a threat to their own visions and aspirations. Therefore, you need to guard your dreams with all your ability and pray to God for guidance. Dream big and work towards its actualization while you guard it against external aggressors continually and continuously. Dreams must be nurtured, especially in God's word, before it can germinate and grow, as well as bear fruit. Unfortunately, many have lived their lives without definite vision. Some have ideas that were not nurtured while many died with their visions- the greatest tragedy in a man's life. The good news is that it is never too late. You can start dreaming from this moment. All you need now is a little direction.

Conclusively, dreams are a product of the mind. It is what you can imagine that you will acquire. When you dream big, nothing can make you small. The only required thing is confidence in yourself and your dream. God has brought each of us here for a reason. Without the purpose that he has placed in your heart, you merely exist. It is what is called the living dead. No matter how great you may want to become, or have already become, if you are not working in your designed purpose, you will be like a dead lion. Your life visions can only be actualized when you figure out what your God-given purpose truly is. So, while driving your dreams and visions towards realization, never forget that you are here for a specific reason. As you have dreams for your life and future, remember to dream high. If you do that, I can assure you that the sky is just a starting point for you. The world will hear about you.

FOLLOWING THE LEADER: CLARITY IS THE KEY

When we were kids, most of us played "Follow the Leader." The idea was that we would take turns being the "Leader". In fact, the one who followed the best was to become the next leader. Sometimes that didn't happen. Sometimes the "Leader" wanted to remain the leader and the followers wanted that person to continue on being the leader. Sometimes the "Leader" wanted to continue on being the leader and those following didn't want him to continue on, because they may have felt the person that led wasn't a good leader. So, there was discord; some quit caring if they followed, others purposely quit following, some became confused as to who they were supposed to be following, and some broke off into their own game of "Follow the Leader". Aren't we glad that, as adults, these things don't happen in real life?

But, they do.

A Harris Interactive poll was taken to find out how well organizations function under current leadership. Here are the results which involved interviewing 23,000 working Americans and interpreted by the late Stephen Covey as if these organizations were 11-member sports teams:

Only 4 of 11 players would know which goal was theirs

Only 2 of 11 would care

Only 2 of 11 would know what position they played and what their role was

9 of 11 would, in some way, be competing against their own team, instead of the opponent

With the wealth of leadership training available, why is the leadership in Corporate America and American Politics so lacking? With all of the leadership training on the market, why do organizations ask for new leadership training? Borrowing a Tony Robbins comment about leadership, Robbins said, "A leader is someone that creates breakthroughs. We're living in the most disappointing time in leadership in my history of being here. Why are we disappointed? Because the people we are calling leaders are really followers. Most politicians and even corporate leaders are trying to keep their jobs, so they do what's popular. There's no leadership in following what's popular. Leadership is your capacity to step in when you know it's unpopular, but you know in your soul that it's right and to influence others. In my mind, here's my definition of a Leader: A person of real influence. A person that will not stand for something if they know it's not right.."

Here's my challenge to you; How will you show yourself to be a true Leader? What legacy will you leave that will have an impact on the people you touch and beyond? What are you going to do to change the stats shown above?

I want to look at some areas of life and business to give you some guidance. And, I believe you have to start with your own psychological, convictional, and behavioral systems.

1. Are you congruent in your life? Here's a great test to find out if you are, or not. Are you happy? If you're not happy, then how you see yourself (psychologically) isn't congruent with who you are being. If you're incongruent and not happy, then how can you have a positive impact on those you lead?

2. What do you believe (convictional)? Do you believe you aren't worthy? Not good enough? Not confident enough? Not good-looking enough? Tall enough? Short enough? Skinny enough? Do you believe that other people are only out for a paycheck? Aren't honest? Are lazy? Are stupid? That they will always have more than

you? That others are "lucky" when they find success... and you don't?

3. What does your lifestyle (behaviors) show about you? Do you display anger? Treat other people with disrespect? Give up when things get tough? Look for excuses, instead of solutions? Find someone else to blame things on when a project fails? Always are asking for more resources, rather than being more resourceful?

Once a Leader brings these areas into focus, they then have an opportunity to be a real benefit to the people they lead.

The next area I believe that a real leader will create is a culture that fosters the outcomes they desire and that fits their vision, mission, and values. This may not be the same as the organization with whom they belong. I'll give you a personal example: One point in my military career, I was once the officer in charge of one of the staff sections in the battalion where I worked directly for the battalion commander, who was overall in charge of the entire unit. The commander had created an environement where almost everyone was in fear of her. Subordinate commanders in her charge would throw each other and their own soldiers under the bus to prevent being on the receiving end of her wrath. If you can imagine, it was all about survival in that unit. Soldiers were not being properly taken care of. The morale of the unit was extremely low. Soldiers had very low levels of respect for the leadership in the unit. I had determined that I wanted to help change the culture. I started with my own staff section. When I first got there, I took the time to sit down with every soldier that worked in my section. I asked them questions about what they did in the section. I asked them about their family, their experience, and their goals and desires. This was something that was unusual in that unit. Just from doing that small thing it caused the soldiers and NCOs to respect me as a leader. It caused my section to run smoothly and the morale was the highest it had ever been. Needless to say, this caught the attention of everyone in the unit, including the battalion commander. She admired me for the way I ran my section. Here's why: I never shied away from her when she tried to intimidate me the way she did everyone. I would stand tall and face her like the leader I was, in my own right. The thing is, I didn't do that just for myself. I often did it in defense of my own soldiers and NCOs. If something was wrong in my section, I always took the blame. I wanted to protect my people. Oftentimes, the commander knew what I was doing, and she respected me for it. Not only that, my soldiers and NCOs respected me for it, as well. Eventually, I had become a trusted agent of the battalion commander, as well as many other officers and soldiers in my unit. Over time, the culture of the unit changed. Sometimes, it just takes one person to take a stand and be authentic to change a culture from negative to positive.

So, what will you do to create the culture around you that drives extraordinary outcomes? You must first have a vision that you are passionate about and that is bigger than yourself. It must be something that others want to contribute to and be a part of, something that will change something for the better. What's your mission for the people you're leading, the reason for them being gathered together? What values do you and the people you lead hold on to? When you create this culture, it brings a great deal of clarity. Let me give you a few examples:

> You will know what projects you will take and which ones you won't
> You will know which people you will engage and bring on the team and which ones you won't
> You will know which people will stay on the team and which ones will not
> You will know what behaviors will be promoted and cultivated... and what behaviors won't be tolerated

There are many more areas, but you get the idea.

As you fully consider all of this information, you will discover that clarity is the key. Clarity about yourself (psychological, convictional, and behavioral), clarity about your purpose, and clarity about your desired outcomes and the culture that will make them achievable. With this clarity, here are what your stats will look like from the aforementioned poll:

Only 11 of 11 players will know which goal was theirs

Only 11 of 11 will care

Only 11 of 11 will know what position they play and what their role is

0 of 11 will, in some way, be competing against their own team, instead of the opponent

YOU ARE THE ONE TO DEVELOP THE LEADER IN YOU!

Leadership is the act of guiding and directing others to achieve a goal. In essence, there has to be a person that directs or guides the others, a leader, and a pilot who knows how to get to the destination. Now, a leader does not just wake up one day and proclaim or emerge as a leader. Just like a baby, a baby does not start walking immediately when he is born; it takes stages like sitting, crawling, and standing. I also liken it to the trees that produce fruits. After planting, it does not just spring up and bear fruit, it goes through phases. So, it takes a lot of things to be in place to unfold as a real leader and be at an advantage. Any leader who can understand this will find it easy to thrive as a great leader before he even realizes it. A leader is out to make positive impact and influence others to become reputable leaders too, and you can not do that when you do not have the skills or know what it takes to be one.

You have to be competent to earn respect or even inspire others. This is why a leader has to be patient, disciplined and should do what it takes to achieve his or her aim. Because, if you are not patient enough, and do not understand that you have more work than others, you won't acquire the skills you need, and will definitely lack the confidence. Therefore, in order to develop your leadership you need self-study, education, training and experience.

No one knows you better than you do and for you to grow and become a great leader, you must understand yourself better. Understand your body, your strengths, weaknesses, what makes you, what you can do best, etc. Self mastery will actually help you map out your goal and how to achieve it. It will help you improve on yourself, your virtue, and quality. It is one of the big steps to make, because then you will have a principle that guides you, and from there comes your success. You have made the act or process of acquiring general knowledge, developing the powers of reasoning and judgment.

To influence others or bring about a change, or even lead your generation, education is the foundation. It is the fundamental power you need to crush any competition and be at an advantage. It doesn't have to end at a certain stage, it should be a lifestyle; study, be enlightened and no one will match you. Don't think you are an expert and that you know everything. Be open-minded because, learning, for a leader, never ends. As life-long learners, we learn and desire to know more to help us lead more effectively.

Training is the process of developing what you have learned. To be a great leader, it is not just about learning, but putting it into practice, developing what you already know. Training is necessary because, then you will be able to add in your generated ideas and also generate new ideas while practicing. It is a continuous process which leads to greater experience and success.

Our memory consolidates things that happen, and when the same thing happens again, it clicks and we can often predict the outcome or know the solution for the situation. To be an effective leader, gain experience and let all of it count because with that, your skills as a leader will dramatically improve. It will make you ever-ready for every situation. See beyond what others see and every idea should count. Don't push away or shy away from any situation. Face it! Be a problem solver and be active. With every problem solved, you gain more experience and nothing takes your confidence away. In essence, you are not born a leader, but efficiently made. It's a continuous process that takes time and effort. Great leaders make other leaders too, but to do that, you need great wisdom and general knowledge to be competent and have an advantage wherever you find yourself. So if you want to develop your leadership skills, build yourself, and you will in turn, build others. Remember, you are the one who has to develop the leader in you and lead others.

LEADERS FOLLOW THEIR DREAMS

"There's no reason to be the richest man in the cemetery. You can't do any business from there." This was a quote from Harland Sanders who became known by the world as The Colonel Sanders of KFC. He was a man who followed his dream after numerous failed attempts. He never gave up and continued to pursue his dream when so many people had given up on him. Colonel Sanders dreamed of a unique empire, the likes of which the world had never witnessed, and not only created a business empire, but a personal lifestyle that clearly identified the man with his dream. What can and should leaders learn from Colonel Sanders?

There can be no leadership without an individual having a dream for what they would like to achieve for their organization. The most effective leaders have a clear cut vision created by this dream, and this drives them to motivate others to share their dream. Effective leaders appear to have amazing amounts of energy that drives them to believe in their personal mission. This dream, when it comes to leadership, generally amounts to someone's view of what could and should be, and what would happen if the correct combination of ingredients are stirred together, just like the Colonel's secrecy recipe. Dreams are generally positive projections of a leaders vision for the organization, and the best leaders are always dreamers.

Of course, one of the most famous leaders who spoke of a dream was the late Dr. Martin Luther King, Jr., in his "I have a dream" speech. Dr. King's dream, of course, was of a color-blind world, where all men would be treated equally regardless of race, creed or religion. Undoubtedly, this dream drove Dr. King to tirelessly pursue the civil rights movement, and it was that dream that many other great leaders are often measured against.

Prospective leaders should ask themselves what their dream is. How do they envision that dream impacting their actions, and where do they hope that dream takes them, and thus permits them to steer their organization under their guidance and leadership? However, no matter how great one's dream is, it is essential for a leader to "wake up" and transform the dream into reality. These leaders must consider their dreams thoroughly and evaluate their actions, by taking certain measures:

1. What action is needed to achieve the positive results envisioned in the dream? How will you make it a reality?

2.   How will you get others to "buy into" your dream? How will you motivate them? Why should they adopt your dream, and take possession of it sufficiently to also make it theirs?

3.   Is the dream one that is truly in the best interests of the organization? A dreamer must be certain that his actions are not merely self-serving, but truly are in his organization's best interest.

4.   Why does the leader feel his dream is so important to the organization?

5.   How has the leader taken personal "possession" of the dream?

If we want an organization to flourish, we need to encourage dreamers to be effective leaders. Let's all "own our dreams" and belong to organizations that help our dreams become reality.

HOW TO FIND AND CREATE A DREAM FOR YOUR LIFE

Believe it or not, there are some people who don't dream about their future. They aren't trying to become superheroes and they aren't trying to retrieve dead dreams, they just don't dream at all. That part of their subconscious which is designed for revealing creative information during a resting state, has collapsed with negative thoughts and defeat; or worse yet, the subconscious has been totally suppressed. This can easily happen when all one meditates on during the day is past failures; or when one abuses his or her mind by filling up on entertainment that clogs the subconscious with other people's dreams.

Let's say that you have believed all the negative talk that says you were good for nothing and will always be a loser. Rather than standing up and fighting, you took those negative words and replayed them in your head until they consumed you. Now, you find yourself in the very place THEY said you'd be. For you this was a self-fulfilling prophecy. Then there are those when after hearing negative talk retreated and hid by bombarding their heads with worthless entertainment or what I like to call mental junk food. These escape artists would rather attach themselves to an iPhone, television or cheap thrill books than finding a way to be successful themselves. They are called air-heads or space cadets, but in reality some people cannot cope with the tough situations of life. For others, this type of behavior is just a symptom of something more dangerous going on inside of them that could lead to depression and maybe even something more serious.

If any of the previous descriptions seem to match your life, I have good news! There is hope for your life. You are exactly the person I am seeking to help. I have been where you are, so let me throw you this lifeline, but you have to want to change your situation or what I am about to share will not work for you. So, are you ready to become your own Dream Weavers? Let's get started!

Set aside a notebook and label it "My Dreams for My Life." If you don't have a notebook handy, then get a piece of paper and on the top line write "My Dreams for My Life", and underline this title. Then get a sheet of paper for each of the following categories and begin evaluating your interests as follows:

1   The thing(s) I always wanted to do since I was a kid.

2   The thing(s) that I wanted to do for which I didn't have enough money, or education, or courage, etc (be specific).

3   The thing(s) I wanted to do, but allowed my family, friends and even my negative self-talk, to kill the idea(s).

4   The thing(s) I dream about doing in secret for fear that someone will find it stupid or impractical.

5   The positive passion in my heart that is pulling me toward a particular area of employment or education or charity work, and I can't shake this feeling.

6   The passions that anger me and move me to want to do something about a situation and make it better.

7   The thing(s) that would make me the proudest to accomplish for myself, my family and the world.

These seven categories will get you started, and, this is just the beginning. Once you have narrowed the list down to the thing(s) that you feel motivated and obligated to carry out, then start doing more research on how to get them done. Don't worry about what you don't have, put those things on a separate list, but begin with the things you are qualified to do right now, and one by one, tackle the things you don't have in creative ways. For example, you may need special training for your dream and don't have money. Find someone that owns a business in that area and offer to work a few hours a week in exchange for gaining the skills you need for where you are going. Also look for free resources on the Internet and at the local public libraries and community colleges in your area. You'll be amazed at how much is available and within reach of anyone who takes time to search.

Now, the next time those negative tapes began to play in your head, just press the pause button and use your dream list to record a new, positive stream of information flow to your mind and heart. Find special people who will support your dreams and speak positively over your life. Affirmation and support are great if you can find it, but if you don't find it, learn how to affirm yourself with positive self-talk.

Plato called necessity the "mother of invention", and I would add that the dreams we possess are the seeds of the Creator and Father God who placed them within the womb of our hearts, not only to nourish, but to bring forth healing and prosperity to us and our families in the form of brilliant schemes and inventions (according to Proverbs 8:12 KJV) that will ultimately change the world.

MY DREAM AND WHERE I AM

For every person, there is that one dream which matters the most. The thought of it brings a smile to the face, a renewed hope and most definitely (in some cases) brings forth the determination needed in pursuing that dream.

I remember growing up, my dream was to become a big time businessman. It was fascinating to see the men in their suits with the brief case going on about their business. As young as my mind was at the time, 1 always thought to myself, "Wouldn't it be great to be a business owner?" I never knew about the difficulties that came with the job. I just loved my dream and the innocence that came with it. For me, what mattered most was making a lot of money, but also being able to put smiles on the faces of others and making their day. I always felt like I would make the kind of money that would allow me to be a blessing to others. It might not bring a permanent solution to their problems, but a ray of hope and light is always appreciated in the midst of darkness. A lot of people thought it was just a mere childish dream that would only last for a while, but believe me, it was more than that. Making a difference in someone's life has and will always be my dream. You might be wondering if 1 became a business owner. To answer that question, 1 would say YES.

I am living my dream. I am living my passion. I am doing what l love. l have not fully reached where l am aiming yet, because I feel like there is still a lot for me to do. My passion lies with children as well as experienced adults, alike. I like to see people be successful in general, which is one of the motivating factors for writing this book. While I can say I am living my dream and working in my passions now, it was not a smooth and easy journey. There have been a lot of bumps and hard lessons along the way. This means that in life, sometimes things won't always go the way we plan them, but there are many ways to achieve your dream. With the passion to make a difference in the lives of others, l figured that l would be a person who could share life lessons that could potentially help others to avoid some of the mistakes that I made and become great leaders.

Basically, l have spent some time talking about my dream, its aim, and the direction l took. Now let us focus on dreams in general. There is nothing wrong with dreaming, but there is a lot wrong with remaining in dreamland. Technically speaking, when a person dreams, that means they are either fast asleep or day dreaming. Either way, you never get anything done in these two instances. It is every individual's responsibility to get up and do something about that dream because if we do not work towards the dream becoming a reality, we will only live it through other people who took the initiative.

There are three steps that every individual should take towards seeing their dream become a reality. We will discuss each step separately.

1. Positive Thinking

Many of us have big dreams with the wrong mindset. Instead of believing that you can do it no matter what, you focus on the distance between you and your dream. What this does is blur your vision and block you from seeing a positive outcome. This all starts with the type of mindset we uphold. I do not argue that there are those who work to put us down through negative talk and discouragements, but then, what would life be without them?

Be the Master of your mind, trusting God to guide your thoughts so that they do not tread in the wrong direction. You are what you think and every time a negative thought pops up, you need to think of a positive thought to neutralize it. The negative forces of the universe want to steal every bit of self-confidence and faith you have.

When you have a positive outlook on life, you cease to be anxious about tomorrow because you know that you were called to do this thing. You have faith in the one who holds your life and in turn, start seeing yourself where you want to be even before you have reached that destination. Your mind harnesses your dreams, nurture it in the right direction with the right ingredients to receive the intended result. Deny negative thinking and believe that you can, and definitely you will.

Going back to the title of this section which says "My dream and where 1 am," a lot of people are not living their dreams, but still wish they could. Some people have already given up on them. It would not hurt to take time to reflect on what could have possibly gone wrong. Did you have the right mind set? Did you guard your thoughts so that they were not be wavered by evil thoughts? Not everyone's 'now' was determined by negative thinking. As we discuss further steps, some will discover they fall short of one of the steps or all of the steps.

The next step towards bringing a dream to life is to be a risk taker. Simply say, 'to overcome fear'.

2. Overcome Fear

If l am to brutally describe fear, then l would liken its effects to that of a taser gun which has paramount effects that incapacitate the whole body and bring nothing, but pain when the mind is conscious. Fear restricts you from moving forward, from progressing and budding out. It brings you to a complete stand still and robs you of any development. That being said, fear is a part of us and we should face it which is termed courage.

When we allow fear to dominate the major part of our lives, it becomes crippling because instantly we are waving off success as well as the opportunity to see what exists on the other side. If life revolved around 'what ifs' then its fullest potential would not be explored. When you hesitate and over analyse things, you allow yourself to take a step back from implementing your dream. Every success story followed a series of steps with which bumps and curves were met along the way, but the individuals never gave up. Take risks and learn from the outcome!

Fear incapacitates us beyond our own imagination and this kind of fear which hinders production is 'destructive fear.' If we trust in GOD, He will be able to grant us the courage we need to face our fears and reverse its effects, which include, but are not limited to, time wasted and limited production.

Godly fear; however, actually enhances us as opposed to the destructive fear that we allow to hinder us. Every minute, every second counts and is essential in allowing every individual to reach unimaginable heights. Today is what you have and tomorrow is what you hope for. Live for today, because now is the only time you have. Break out of your shell and make the most of today as if it were your last day on earth. How it turns out, just accept the outcome and that way you will not live to regret not trying at all. Devise the next step from what you have learned! Don't stop just keep going!

Personally, I used to have a terrible fear of speaking in public. But you see, if I had let this fear direct me, I would never have been able to do what I do now. I am a leadership coach, trainer and public speaker who spends a lot of time speaking to the public. In my line of work, I also host my own radio talk show where I talk about leadership. One way as an individual to overcome fear would be to surround yourself with positive people. I had family and friends who have supported me in my search for greatness. Honestly, it was not easy for me to overcome my fear of public speaking. It took a lot of time and practice for me to get to the point where I could function during a speech or be able to talk without shaking noticeably. I still get a little nervous today, but now it's different. It's the kind of nervous energy that I have because I know I am about to speak to an audience and share myself with them in the hopes that I will say something that will change someone's life. I still have my support network that encourages me along the way.

Such people play a pivotal role in our lives because the drive behind their support is seeing us succeed - getting out of that destructive dominating shell. That fear is still a part of me, but I can proudly say, every time I step on a stage, I face a fear that diminishes just a little bit more than before. Now I embrace that nervous energy. It has become a familiar sensation that I have every time I get ready to do something great. I'm always looking at the big picture – changing the lives of others for the better.

Another technique would be to keep motivating yourself with positive talk like, " Everything will be ok" or "All is well." "I can do this," even if you are shaking in your boots. You will be amazed at how far you can go with positive talk and a positive mental attitude. By now, the connection between step one and step two should be becoming more evident.

3. Observe

When we take note of what happens in our surroundings, we absorb a lot of content. Not all of it may be of use, but all the information that we can use for our own benefit is worth the time. There are a lot of people out there who have achieved greatness through adversity that we can learn a great deal from for our own benefit.

It is every individual's responsibility to take time to study how others became successful; how they achieved their goals and dreams. There are things that person A did that person B did not. Combined together, this can give you an overview of how you should go about achieving your dream. Be a diligent reader. You know and learn more when you research more. Be slow to judge and spend more time trying to understand and conceptualize things for yourself. Previously, we talked about taking risks, but do not mistake this for being irrational and too impulsive. Give thought to what you want to do, how you intend to go about it and then move to action. When you act upon impulse, there is a good chance that the first step you take towards achieving your goal will not be a success. This will not be because the step was wrong, but possibly because it was not carefully planned and implemented strategically.

THE DREAM KILLERS

Earlier, I shared a topic concerning "passion" with you...

I just want to piggy-back on that a little further because even with being passionate about a goal or cause, there's another added mental factor you must have to make it all the way through, and that's perseverance.

Perseverance is a trait that can be cultivated if you find that you don't have enough of it. The initial step to developing it is to eliminate it's five greatest enemies, which I want to share with you now.

1. **A Lifestyle of Giving up** - A little boy had been promised ice-cream by his grandfather if he was good while they were out shopping. After a few hours, the little boy asked "How much longer will it be?" "Not too much longer", the grandfather replied." "We just have one more stop we need to make." "I don't know if I can make it grandpa." The little boy then replied, "I can be good. I just can't be good long enough." When we are kids and we don't follow through on a task, people often give us a break. That's to be expected. Children tend to jump from one activity to another and to bounce from idea to idea. Adults can't do that and expect to be

65

successful. If you have the desire to be successful, you need to be consistent and persistent. Opportunities without persistence will be lost. If you have a habit of giving up, you need to overcome it to be successful.

2. **Believing That Life Should Be Easy Just like a marriage** - There will be times you'll feel like giving up, but hanging in there and continuing to try is often the way to make it through. Do you want to know the biggest characteristic that separates those from reaching their goals versus those that don't?........expectations. Those that don't expect to succeed right away, and view their failures as a reason to recommit and a reminder to refocus on their goals with more determination, experience a great deal more success in their lives than those that want success immediately.

3. **Believing That Success Is A Destination** - So you've reached a goal......now what? Most people, once reaching a milestone in a given opportunity will suddenly have the attitude that they have arrived. They simply lose that "hunger." If you think you've arrived, then you're in trouble. As soon as you think you no longer need to work hard to make progress, you'll begin to lose ground.

4. **A Lack Of Resiliency** - What is it? Think of it metaphorically speaking as a twig with a fresh, green living core. When twisted out of shape, it bends, but it doesn't break; instead it springs back and continues growing. It's an excellent description of how we must be if we desire to persevere through adversity and make the most of the talent we have. We must not become dry, brittle, and inflexible. And we must have the mindset of bouncing back, no matter how we may feel. "You can't get much done in life if you only work on the days you feel good." ~ Jerry West

5. **Lacking A Vision** - Everything that is created is actually created twice. First it's created mentally; then it's created physically. Where does that mental creation come from? The answer is vision. People who display perseverance keep a larger vision in mind as they toil away at their craft or profession. They see in their mind what they want to create or do, and they keep working toward it as they labor. A very good friend of mine is a fashion designer who quite often shares her projects that she's worked on or in the process of working on as pictures on notebook paper. All of these are works of incredible designs that started with a picture in her mind! You have

to see the end from the beginning and it starts with a vision.

Clearing away these five enemies of perseverance is a preliminary step to becoming all that you can be and developing perseverance. Proper thinking always precedes action!

ACTION

TAKE ACTION AND BECOME YOU

It's time to make a difference. Life is too short and you can't continue to hold on to reasons of why you can't get ahead to accomplish your own dreams. Excuses are tools of the incompetent and will get you nowhere and it's time to be the one to step out and step up. If you've been brought up around a family who has done nothing but settle, be the one who steps out of that comfort zone to make a change.

There's nothing wrong with shaking things up a bit. Who knows? You might inspire other family members to do the same. It's not too late to break the cycle. Show the kids of the future that life can be better and that they can have the finer things in life if they strive and work hard for them. Things don't always come easy and you can't just sit around and wait for them to fall into your lap. Start today in taking action for yourself. Don't just say to yourself, "I'm going to make things different!" Develop a detailed plan to guarantee that you'll make things different and then FOLLOW IT!

This is a brand new day, so introduce everyone to a brand new YOU! If you've been that one who was the procrastinator, demonstrate your leader qualities and become the "action taker". If you've been that one who was always insecure with yourself, put the insecurities aside so that you can pursue those dreams that you've wanted to achieve for so long. Make a commitment to yourself that you will not allow any more excuses and unveil the real "You" by delivering on the potential that God has created within you. You already know what it is you want and now it's your time to begin realizing it!

Begin paying close attention to those that you keep around you. Sometimes in order to get ahead, we have to reach ahead. It's okay and oftentimes, even desirable to find yourself a mentor or someone to coach you so that you are able to stay on track towards accomplishing your goals. When selecting this person, be sure you are learning from someone who has ALREADY "done it" and who really cares about your success! When someone has already "been there and done that", they'll be able to relate to your struggles and share their own experiences that you might be able to relate to. This can allow you to sidestep some of the pitfalls that they went through. All of this equates to one thing, you'll reach your goals faster and with fewer bumps and bruises.

It's also important to increase your knowledge. When I first set out to become an entrepreneur I spent a lot of time online until the wee hours of the morning (sometimes I still do). I didn't care about the time because when you are on a mission to achieve your goals, and of course doing something that you enjoy doing, you won't mind putting in the time and effort to achieve the results that you are after. So when it came time to do my research, I jotted down many notes and bookmarked many pages on my computer. I always kept a journal with me as well, because when an idea came, I wanted to be sure to record it. Read enough books and you'll find enough nuggets to make a bar. When I came across a book or books that had too much information to write down, those were the books that I ended up purchasing.

I tell people that we sometimes have to watch who we keep in our circle when we're on a mission to improve our personal and professional lives. Your friends might feel as if you are acting differently towards them because you don't do the same things you did before. You'll have some friends who will work that 9-5 work week and during their off time, they want to do just that...BE OFF. To some, the party's on! Or to others, they just want to relax and do absolutely nothing because...THEY'RE OFF! And for them, that's ok.

When I was in the military world, I not only worked towards advancing within my field of expertise, but during my "off" time, I worked even harder to advance my own business aspirations and personal goals for myself and my family.

Starting today, be inspired to do what it takes to grow in life, and not just go through life!

POWERFUL TIPS FOR SUCCESS THAT WORK

If you want to be successful and achieve all your dreams and goals, this is the right book for you to read. What you are about to discover here are 5 easy and powerful tips for success that you cannot miss.

Before you get to know these tips for success, you have to first understand what makes most people fail to live their dreams and achieve their goals. The most common reason people fail to accomplish what they want in their lives is because they are not determined and committed enough with what they want in their lives. As long as you have these two powerful forces in you, just follow through these 5 tips for success...

1. Always think about what you want to accomplish in your life all the time. What you focus on grows. You have to keep thinking about what you want to achieve in your life. If you want to be a millionaire, think about the life of becoming a millionaire all the time. This is the most fundamental step to manifesting your dreams.

2. Next, you will have to be clear about what you want and set a specific goal for it. Write down what you want to

achieve in your life on a piece of paper right now. Remember, you have to be as specific as possible and include a deadline for your goal. The reason you do this is that you want to have a constant reminder of the goal.

3. Once you have written down your goals on a piece of paper, take another piece of paper and write down all the steps and action tasks that you must do in order to make your goals come true. You have to break down all your goals into small and achievable steps, then you can take action and move toward your goals everyday.

4. Another one of the tips for success is that you have to keep on learning and improving in your related field. For example, if your goal is to be a multi-millionaire, you will have to read and learn about how to manage your finances and how to create wealth. It is only by learning that you will transform from ordinary to extraordinary.

5. Finally, take action every single day according to your plan. You have to keep the momentum going by constantly taking action everyday. Most people fail because they procrastinate and they find it hard to build up the drive that will get them going again.

ACTIONS ARE THE BRICKS OF REALITY

Throughout human history and culture, selected individuals from all different walks of life have cultivated the ability to live life to their highest potential. They live by the truth that we are not human beings having a spiritual experience, but spiritual beings having a physical one. They have clearly seen that our essential nature is that of a producer; we are born to produce and the choice lies only in consciously choosing what we wish to produce as our own reality. These are people who have fully accepted the truth that they are not going to live forever. They have decided to live life fully - in every moment. They have become believers in action.

If you want to lose weight, all the knowledge and statistics of different diets will be of no use unless you actually begin to implement them. If you wish to become a millionaire, all the money making secrets are useless unless action begins on them. If you want to get fit again, it's more important to get to the gym regularly than to study countless magazines about what you need to do.

People who achieve what they want are acutely aware that of all the wonders and mysteries of our universe, nothing is as wonderous as the human mind, for that is where the creation of reality begins. The famous philosopher Henry

Skolimowski wrote, "Of all the gifts of evolution, the mind is the most precious. Yet we have allowed it to become something other than what is truly is. Much pollution is poured into your mind daily. This garbage has trivialized your existence. It is the cause of anxieties and confusion that does not allow you to think properly and act appropriately."

These words mirror the truth proclaimed by all the wisdom traditions of the world. The human mind can either be a dumping ground or treasure trove - a faithful friend or a dangerous enemy. We can use our intelligence to create or to destroy, to enhance our existence or to demean it, to fulfil our highest potential or to live an unfulfilled life.

All the high achievers of this world know that success in any area of life is not simply an external activity but an inner awareness as well. It begins with how we use our mind. All successful people share a common mind-set that differentiates them from the masses. It is this mindset that gets translated into action which goes on to make things real in the external world. Success and achievement begins inside them, in their inner thinking, long before it becomes real in the external world through their actions for all to see.

It is amazing to note that invariably all of such elevated spirits believe in action. They are conscious of their roles as producers and they create willingly and knowingly. They clearly understand and believe in the counsel of the Dhammapada: "However many words you read, however many you speak, what good will they do if you do not act upon them?"

They know that nothing changes unless action is taken. They know that action is the building block of reality. They are people of action, and inspire others to create - through action. Once they've decided what they want, they go into everything completely, fully and totally - without holding themselves back.

Such people know that in their action lies their power, and that action begins in thoughts we carry around in our mind. They know that the choice of how they want to react to a happening, any happening, is up to them. They are masters of their own attitude to life, and everything in it. They choose to act, rather than to react to stimulus of different kinds in their life.

Here are some unique character traits of those who believe action changes reality...

People of action jump into action. They know that wisdom turns into strength only if it is followed up with action. To learn how to swim, you must get wet. They understand that any weakness voluntarily faced and met is the same as greeting a greater strength.

People of action walk one step at a time. They are not too concerned about how much there is to do, or how impossible some of the tasks seem. They focus on getting one thing done at a time, again and again. They are aware that the journey of a thousand miles begins with a single step. And the most beautiful tapestry begins and ends with one of ten thousand individual threads.

People of action know that the time is always 'Now'. They know that you can't change the mind of the person you are later. There is no later, it's always now or never. This moment, ever-present, ever-powerful, is before them, and it has limitless potential. The time to change their destiny is 'NOW.'

People of action follow through with focused actions. They know that once you've taken the first step, you'll gain some direct knowledge about what is working and what isn't. Then you can modify your plans. As experience and wisdom increases from each creative effort, so does their ability to more quickly and accurately evaluate the merits and weaknesses of each action they take.

One of the keys is building momentum - gradually adding energy and force to each new result they want to create. Once they've arrived at a creative goal, they clearly acknowledge it, and then look ahead for the next creation. As the Swiss psychologist Carl Jung stated "Your vision will become clear only when you can look to your own heart. Who looks outside, only dreams; who looks inside, also awakes."

The achievers of this world know the powerful truth, "inch by inch, life is a cinch. Yard by yard, life is hard". Success is always built one action at a time, over a long time.

A Zen Master once told his student, "If you know but do not do, you do not know!" I am prone to agree with the statement, "If you continue to do what you've always done, you will continue to get what you've always gotten! To change what you're getting, you have to change what you're doing."

Nothing is created without action. Wisdom lays the foundation, but it is action that finally changes life and the future. This is the unspoken secret of all creation and change in life.

5 KEYS TO EXECUTIVE ACTION FOR SUCCESS

Do you want to succeed as an entrepreneur? Do you want to succeed at making money online, as a parent, in your spiritual life? Do you want to transform your way of being, seeing, and operating in the world?

To succeed, excel, gain mastery, or get started in any area of your life, you must take action. In spite of your fear, insecurities, challenges, or lack of resources, you must take action. However, there is the kind of action that produces the desired results (executive action), and then there is the kind of action that amounts to inaction.

Thinking about it certainly won't do it. Reading about it won't do it. Taking classes won't do it. Planning won't do it either. Your success might start with any of these, and each of them is a necessary kind of action to take, when getting started, but without executive action, it will not happen. Period.

What is executive action? Executive action is action that is suited and effective for reaching your goals. I've seen too many cases of people making preparation, doing research, creating plans, and talking about what they're going to do to pursue a goal, like start a business or lose weight, for example, only to see the whole endeavor fizzle and dissolve. Then it's never mentioned again, until the next big thing. I've done it myself. I know what that's like. It ain't fun. Action - consistent, focused action, i.e., executive action - is what makes it happen.

Try staring at a pen and use all your mental powers to cause that pen to come to your hand. The pen won't budge. Stare at your screen (or your blank sheet of paper) and will the words to appear on the blank space. The screen will stay blank.

Stare in the mirror and visualize your body perfectly muscular and tight (assuming it's not). Stare at it for 12 hours a day. Do you think that will get you in shape? Mental powers, will, and visualization are great; however, without executive action those things amount to nothing.

So what are the keys to executive action?

5 Keys To Executive Action

1. Take only one step at a time –

Take the first step and focus only on the first step. Then, when that step is completed, take the second step with complete focus. If you focus on the whole journey/process, it can be easy to become discouraged.

It's like eating a watermelon - sure it's huge, but you eat the whole thing one bite at a time.

2.   Act in spite of your fears -

As a combat veteran, I can tell you that fear is constantly with you, but if the fear paralyzes you, you're a goner. If you keep moving, execute your orders, you have a fighting chance. It's no different when you pursue your goals. Action keeps the fear on the sidelines, not front and center.

3.   When you act, keep your vision in mind -

This is powerful. The human mind is a goal-striving machine, much like guided missiles. Guided missiles have a target programmed into them and when they are launched they head for the target. As the missile flies toward the target, it is constantly going off-course and corrects itself as it moves forward until it strikes its target. The missile 'sees' its programmed target the entire time and this is how it corrects itself. Keeping your vision/goal in mind as you act guides and empowers your actions all the way to success.

4. **Stay in action -**

When you ride a 2-wheeled bicycle, you must stay in motion to maintain your balance. Once you stop your forward motion, you lose your balance and fall over. It is the same when working towards your goal. You must stay in action to keep the drive toward success going. Stop and you are sure to fall or fail.

5. **Avoid staying busy -**

There's a big difference between staying busy and remaining in (executive) actions, which are focused efforts toward your goal; staying busy is unfocused acts with no real goal or purpose. Executive actions are executed according to plan; staying busy has no plan. Actions are about progress; staying busy is about feeling as if you are making progress.

Again, you must take executive action - consistent, focused action that does not end until you reach your goal. Then you can rest... until the next action toward the next goal is called for. It's all about advancing and experiencing yourself as an empowered, creative being.

ADD ACTION TO YOUR DREAMS

You should dare to dream the impossible. Throughout history, man has continued to keep on doing what has been thought to be impossible prior to the breakthrough. The Wright brothers invented something that was not created to fly naturally. Today we call it the airplane.

Prior to this invention, people thought it was impossible for a piece of metal to be suspended in mid-air, let alone into the heavens. As you dream, add action, because dreaming alone will not get you the results that you see in your dreams.

If you have dreams of seeing a better world, by a new invention or simply by improving an already existing service or product, then truly you are on your way to make your dream a reality.

There is simply no excuse for any of us not to have a dream. Every human born of man is endowed with the ability to dream; to imagine, to envision the miraculous. No one can say for sure or even give a prediction of the heights to which you can soar, and no one besides you, can look beyond your horizon.

You need to spread your wings and fly to heights through your dreams, imaginations and actions. Go wild! Stretch yourself! See yourself breaking through any barriers! Astound yourself - propel and catapult your ideas, your visions! Let them take shape and form. Resonate and run with them. Learn to dream. Think the unthinkable and reach for the unreachable.

Have you got dreams of being the next president, the next super entrepreneur, the next and best whatever? Hey, it is all within your reach! In fact, you are born with it. It is inscribed in your genetic code. Let your dreams guide you. Let them show you the way - step by step. Let your visions and dreams of your future reflect now in your lifestyle, in the choices that you make here and now.

I fully support Daniel Webster who said: "There is always room at the top." There is always room at the top since less people have dreams of reaching there. They literally settle at the bottom of the ladder where it takes no effort to dream or become anything of significance. There are groups of people who stay awake to accomplish their dreams whilst others merely sleep with theirs. May your story be different. May it be said of you amongst your peers that you always had a dream, a vision far greater than yourself and you achieved it, because there is great genius in dreaming!

Normally when you have those unimaginable dreams, people will not believe in them. They will try to tell you how impossible your dreams are and how so many people have failed trying to reach their dreams. Listen to what a wise man said when he first heard the word impossible! His amazing response was this: "Never let me hear that foolish word again!"

Do not listen to the nay-sayers. See them as the little chicken who always runs around saying "the sky is going to fall on everybody one of these days," subtly discouraging and putting fear in their victims. For everyone who doubts you and tells you that you will fail, try twice as hard to prove them wrong.

POWER

POWER OF THE MIND - THINK YOUR WAY TO SUCCESS

The power of the mind is awesome. Though the mind's power is unconquerable, it brings many wonders in a person's life. The power of the mind has enabled people to predict the future, do the most dangerous things in the world, perform miraculous healing as well as mind-over-matter phenomenon.

What is in your mind governs your life - your thoughts, your judgment, how you think about a given situation, even your past experiences and memories. The conscious mind may take charge of the very important functions of your brain, but there is also the subconscious mind that also affects your behavior and beliefs in life.

Controlling Your Health

When it comes to health, we may often become very dependent on medicines and all the modern-day medical procedures available. Sometimes we call them miracles but the mind has its own way of healing the physical body. Stress for example, has been a common culprit in the many illnesses we tend to get from our busy everyday lives, but it is also one thing that can be well taken care of by the power of the mind. Dieting for example, has been a trend almost around the world, and many people find it hard to stick to their diet plans. Of course, your mind has something to do with all this, and behavior control is one technique that uses mind power over dieting.

Controlling your Life

Indeed, the powers of your mind can control your life the way you want it to be. Several techniques have been explored to make good use of the powers of the mind in thinking your way out of your problems, depression, tiredness, emotions, and in promoting mental health. Meditation has been known, not only as a spiritual practice, but also as a tool to cultivate the mind's power to concentrate, connect with your subconscious, find joy and even help in solving everyday problems as well as providing means for self-discovery. Hypnosis, on the other hand, has its own health benefits and is widely used in dealing with mental and emotional problems. The powers of the subconscious, shown in hypnosis, often play a big role in psychotherapy, and is often a proof of the amazing powers of the mind.

Your Conscious and Subconscious Mind

We often think that success in life comes from our ability to make good decisions, taking risks, and the great efforts we put into it. Indeed, these are essential parts of achieving our goals in life, but there may be times that we think we have done so much about it, yet we are still stuck in the same place. In dieting for instance, some people think they really wanted to lose weight, so they tell themselves to stick to the diet plan and resist the urge to pick up that creamy, chocolaty dessert. But at times, our imagination comes into play. Is it our subconscious pushing us toward our old eating habits again?

Great powers of the mind may come from our subconscious, thus if we know how to put these powers to good use, it can truly make great changes in our lives; from breaking bad habits to achieving success in life, these can be attainable with the help of our subconscious.

LEADERSHIP AND POWER - BEING THE BOSS DOESN'T GUARANTEE EITHER

Some people mistakenly associate supervisory positions, or seats of power, with leadership. They presume that these two things are synonymous. While this may be the case sometimes, leadership and power are wholly separate. In reality, the boss may not have all of the power. In fact, they may not be capable of handling it, even if they possess all of it. What do I mean? What is leadership, and what is power? How do they interrelate? How are power and leadership obtained? Let's take a look!

Leadership is the ability to influence others to take action when they might not otherwise be compelled to do so of their own volition. Influence is the key element of leadership. As your influence grows, so does your ability to lead. Demonstrate your leadership ability through action; hands-on is hot, finger pointing is not; provide direction, purpose and motivation.

Power is a more complicated matter. There are five types of power that can be found within the organizational hierarchy, and all of them can be used to accomplish tasks, and perhaps influence others. However, the leader probably will not possess all of these powers...and that's an important concept to understand. It's just as important to realize that having personal possession of all five powers is not essential to being a successful leader. Knowing how to apply these powers is. So, what are the five powers, and how are they used?

Legitimate Power. This is the one power the boss always has, based upon their position in the organization. A first level supervisor, mid-level manager, department head - all have specific power bestowed on them once they accept the supervisory duty position. The boss signs timesheets, approves vacations, assigns work, etc.

Reward Power. This is the capacity to control and manipulate valued resources. For example, the boss may have just received a difficult task to be accomplished with a very short deadline. The boss tells his staff that if they complete the work to standard, and on time, they will have a pass day, or a luncheon for their hard work. This sounds great to the staff, and they get the difficult job done in time. The boss has just used his reward power to influence his workers.

Care must be taken that the boss does not overuse this power, or a backlash effect is possible. Reward appropriately, based on the situation, conditions, and careful consideration. Do not reward for everything. Doing so will diminish this power's effectiveness, and create workers' expectations that they should be rewarded every time they accomplish tasks - difficult or otherwise.

Coercive Power. This is the capacity to control various punishments. Again, this power is usually in the hands of the boss, but could reside with other people in the organization as well. The supervisor could use this power, for example, to give a bad review, disallow time off, or hold back a promotion if a worker is not doing as instructed, expected or otherwise resistant to directions. On the other hand, a worker could also exert coercive power over a supervisor if he was aware of something that could impact the supervisor in a negative way.

Expert Power. This is the strength derived from special skills, expertise, and knowledge. You know this person as the subject matter expert (SME); the Guru; the go-to person. These experts are found up and down the corporate ladder. Be assured that this power is not influenced by pay grade or position. The smart leader seeks out these experts wherever they may be. Knowledge is power, if applied effectively.

Charismatic Power. This influential authority is derived from personal attraction, admiration, or identification with the person. Again, charismatic power may be held by a member of the rank and file; not the boss. You know this person as well. This is someone that others gravitate toward because of their 'aura' or personality. This person may not even have to say much to establish their presence. They could be the good listener with an understanding ear. They may be the silent leader among peers because of their charismatic influence.

Now that you have a basic understanding of what leadership and power are, you also have a good idea of what they are not. It should also now be clear that supervisors do not automatically possess leadership simply because they are granted some power. The supervisory position only gives the individual some authority to accomplish certain tasks and objectives in the organization. This authority, or power; however, does not convey leadership to the individual. It simply puts that person in charge.

A poor supervisor is one who attempts to accomplish work mainly by bossing others around, threatening, strong-arming, or otherwise punishing others into compliance. They do not seek help, they believe they are never wrong, makes no mistakes, and is otherwise inconsistent in word and deed. They have little respect from subordinates and peers alike.

A good supervisor is one who accomplishes work by influencing others to willingly accomplish tasks, achieve goals, and maintain standards. This leader leads by example, seeks help when needed, rewards and punishes fairly. They make mistakes, and acknowledges them. They are respected by co-workers. That's what leadership is about.

There is no quick answer as to how leadership is obtained, but as you already know, some people have great capacity for leadership, while others do not. The seed is planted from your earliest interactions with others; it begins to grow as one matures. In the work force, leadership may blossom with the help of a strong mentor or a seasoned 'veteran' of the organization who takes someone under their wing. Over time, an individuals' leadership quality may improve tremendously if it was based on strong foundations, but for others, a leadership plateau may be reached, and further motivation to improve may not exist. Leadership can be as varied as each individual.

In the end, it doesn't matter if you are a supervisor or not. Leadership is not dependent upon your title or position. Seek out those you admire for their leadership abilities, and follow their example. Improve your own leadership abilities by holding yourself to high standards of conduct and by challenging yourself often. Follow these guidelines, and you have a recipe for leadership success, whilst achieveing your dream through action and power!

SUCCESS IS A PROCESS - DON'T GIVE UP NOW!

Every year at midnight on January 1, I wonder how many people renew the same resolutions they made the New Years before and the New Years before that? Why is it so hard to follow through on the list of things we say are most important to change in our lives? Why do we find ourselves repeating the same mistakes that end us up in the same place of failure year after year? Why do we hit the ground running toward our goals every January 1st and within weeks we are right back in the place we were the previous December 31st?

I think we set ourselves up for both failure and success. Neither of these things just happen to us. One way we set ourselves up for failure is by failing to prepare. Benjamin Franklin once said, "Failing to plan is planning to fail."

Take dieting for example (I don't know about you, but it seems to appear every year on my things-I-want-to-change-this-year list). Walking into the kitchen famished probably is not the best time to decide on a healthy, well-balanced meal. We are more likely to grab the quickest, closest thing in the fridge at that moment. The time to prepare for success in a diet is the night before. Writing out a meal plan for the following day only takes a few minutes, but it can be a great tool for success in reaching weight-loss goals.

I like to think of life as a series of snap-shots. A professional photographer doesn't show up to take wedding pictures with a quick-shot instant camera. The photographer knows you can get a quick picture with an instant camera, but it is not going to be the quality of photograph that a wedding photo deserves. Using the "diet" analogy again, we too can get some quick results with fad diets or pills if we are more concerned with getting it done quickly than getting it done properly. The goal of the photographer is to eventually enable the newly weds to see the beautiful images that are being viewed through the lens. Let's compare the process of reaching our goals to the process of photo development.

First of all, you, the photographer must focus the camera. You must focus on the target/goal. If you do not know exactly where it is you want to go, how will you know when you have arrived? The dictionary defines the word focus as: "clear and sharply defined, a central point of attraction, attention, activity, to concentrate or focus ones attention."

No wonder so many of our resolutions fall by the wayside within days of us making them. How much focus are we giving to achieving our goals? How "clear and sharply defined" have we made our target? Is our goal "The central point of our attraction, attention, and activity?" Can I truly say I'm "concentrating" on my goal at all times? After the photographer has focused his lens, he takes the picture. At that split-second, the shutter opens and the light hits the film creating an exposure of the image onto the film inside.

If we are to achieve our goals, we must also get exposure, and become enlightened on the subject we are aiming for. If the goal is to become the owner of a pizza shop, I need to expose myself to the business of pizza-making; read books, listen to CD's, expose myself to people who have succeeded in doing what it is I have decided to do. This concept applies to any goal we may set for ourselves. Don't just "hope" to reach your goal, get informed and equipped in the subject. Find every resource available to support and encourage your success in this area. If you need to lose weight, find friends or on-line support groups who can hold you accountable and encourage you when you feel like throwing in the towel and running to the nearest ice cream shop to buy all 31 flavors!

Now that the photographer has the image on his film, the film must be "processed" or "developed". There is one and only one reason you may not have reached every single one of your goals yet, and that is because without fail, somewhere along the way you have lost your focus and gave up on the goal during the process of reaching it!

We must submit to the process of development in the area of achieving our goals. Again, when we diet, each temptation we are able to say no to strengthens our resolve and better equips us to greater focus and determination each day. Every time we push ourselves in exercise we stretch our muscles, breaking them down only to find that the result of our pushing and pain produces bigger, stronger muscles than we had before. The process of creating bigger muscles is a hard one and not many people attempt it or follow through with a long-term commitment to exercise, but those who do, reap the benefits and rewards of their effort.

The film can only be developed in a "dark room". How many times have we heard, "It's always darkest just before the dawn?" The dark room is a place of seclusion. It's not a place where people are running in and out and exposing the film. We too, will find times in the process of changes being made in our lives, when we feel alone and secluded from others. They are all going out for pizza and bread sticks and you are left behind with your weight-loss goal and menu planner. Or everyone is out partying all night while you are left at home making phone calls or doing paperwork or reading up on the next step to building a successful business. The dark room of life is not a lively, exciting place but it is a necessary part of the process of success. This is what separates the men from the boys, the dreamers from the achievers. This is when it is easier to follow the path of least resistance. Though some do for a while, not many are willing to sacrifice comfort-zones and put fleshly pleasures on hold for the long haul.

After pouring the right solutions over the film in the dark room, the photographer now finds himself holding what is called "a negative". The negative is an interesting stage of the process of the photograph. When the photographer holds up the negative, the bride, which he witnessed in a snowy white gown, is now dressed in black, and the groom, who was wearing a black tuxedo, is now dressed in white. The negative is the complete opposite of reality. Have you ever been in the 'negative" stage of your life or business? You've been working harder than anyone you know and so far nothing seems to be changing, or worse, you're losing accounts. Or you've stayed on your diet perfectly all week only to step on the scale and find not only did you not lose any weight, you actually gained 2 lbs. This is the "Negative" stage. This is when people, even the ones who seemed to be determined to tough it out before now find they just don't have it in them to continue.

The "negative" stage is the most discouraging and difficult stage of all, but if you can see the "negative" for what it is, you will understand that it is the complete opposite of what is happening in reality! You ARE succeeding, you just have to persevere a little bit longer and you will see on the outside the things that have already started to change on the inside. That negative can never convince that photographer that the bride was actually wearing a black wedding dress. He knows that after the process is finished, he will see things as they actually are!

The photographer then pulls the negative out of the solution and hangs it to dry. Have you ever felt like you've been hung out to dry? Things are not as they appear, not to those who persevere. You see, it's not what you do, it's what you keep on doing that will get you to your goal. Stay focused, continue to do the next right thing and you will without a doubt, reach your goal...hell or high water couldn't keep you from it!

Finally the pictures are fully developed and the photographer presents them to the bride and groom. Everyone sits in awe of the beauty of each captured moment. Each photo is a moment in time that will be forever treasured, yet how many will ever consider the process it took to produce such beautiful images? Few, if any.

Let me remind you that life is not an event. It's a process and so is applying action and power in reaching your goals and dreams. If you will learn to embrace the process, you will eventually find yourself having attained each and every one of your dreams.

SUCCESS COMES WHEN YOU TURN INDECISION AND FEAR INTO POWER AND ACTION

How many times have you had a really great idea or wanted to take a risk and try something new, only to have a little voice inside your head shout: "it won't work!" or "you couldn't possibly do that!" or "what a silly idea!" Everyone, at some point in their lives, has listened to that little voice cautioning them against following a certain action. If you frequently question what you do and think, and veer away from making decisions, then you may be stopping yourself from reaching your fullest potential. You may be slowly squeezing the special creative energy and inspiration inside of you that makes you unique, into a tight knot that needs to desperately unravel.

So what motivates that nagging little voice? What is stopping you from making that important decision or trying something new? One of the most common answers is FEAR. Fear is the greatest single barrier to success in our personal and professional lives. The emotion of fear is intended to warn us of danger and to act as a cautionary tool. It should make us stop and think before taking action.

Fear - The Life Dictator

What fear should not do, is dictate the course of action we take. It should not control our thoughts or relationships with other people, and most importantly fear should not shape who we are or what we want to achieve in our lives. On a conscious or subconscious level, all of us have felt the impact of fear in our lives. Whether it is the fear of making a decision, the fear of failure, the fear of what other people will think, or the fear of success - the consequences are the same.

If left to fester and control our lives, fear eventually leads us to stop trying new things. Our comfort zone pulls tight around us and is rarely pushed further out than it needs to be. We feel stale, lethargic and wonder what is missing in our lives. Our creative energy is replaced with a survival instinct.

On a subconscious level, we start to believe that we are not good enough, or that there is no way possible that we can achieve something new or take a risk. On a conscious level our body and mind responds to being fed negative statements and responds by firmly stating, "I cannot do it!"

What are you afraid of? Have you ever wondered just what you are afraid of? What stops you from taking the next step forward that will keep you on the path of achieving your goals? The reason for most people's fear is buried deep within themselves. A low level of self-confidence and self-esteem makes us feel unhappy about ourselves. Because our thoughts are based on feelings of inadequacy, we set our boundaries and standards very low and achieve little in our lives.

One of the greatest realizations that you may ever experience in your life is that the emotion of fear is part of being human. It is perfectly normal to experience misgivings and doubts! Fear will never go away no matter how self-confident or successful we are.

The key to overcoming our fears is to feel good about ourselves and think positively. We can then begin to use the energy that fear creates positively in our lives. Only then can we turn indecision and fear into power and action. As Franklin Roosevelt said, "We have nothing to fear but fear itself."

BIG THOUGHTS AND BIG ACTIONS MAKE DREAMS COME TO LIFE!

Yes, these two can indeed make your thoughts materialize - even big, seemingly impossible dreams. The process is very straightforward, applying the law of manifestation. It all begins in your mind, with a single thought. If you think small, you get small results. But if you think big, what do you think your results will be? If you think, a small bungalow will be fine as my house, then most likely that is what you will get. On the other hand, if you think you would like a two-story house with a pool and garden, then again, that is what you will most likely get.

Feeling, or passion, follows. This is where the question, "How badly do I want this?" comes in. Also, "What am I willing to do in order to get this?" The answer to this determines your level of commitment. Your passion and commitment also dictate your results. Based on your thought and passion, you set a specific goal with a specific deadline. It is best to write it down as the subconscious mind absorbs it better when you write it down.

Then take big actions that are only worthy of your big thoughts! If you are looking for your dream house, find out how much it costs and how you are going to get it. Think about and visualize your dream house everyday. This activates the law of attraction, where you attract people and events related with what you think about most. Stay alert for "coincidences" from the universe - for example, suddenly meeting an architect or anyone who can help you get that dream house.

Change your actions if needed, until you reach your goal. If for example your sources of income are not enough to finance your dream house, then you may have to change them or add to them. In time, you will reach your goal.

Just keep this formula in mind - big thoughts and big feelings lead to big goals, which in turn lead to big actions, finally leading to big results!

ABOUT THE AUTHOR

Independent certified leadership training, coach and speaker; Amazon Best Selling author, L Wayne Smalls became a resident of Fayetteville, NC. after serving over 25 years of total service in the United States Army; he retired at the rank of Major. He also has an extensive professional educational background in business administration and leadership development.

With a climbing number of progressive books and publications, Wayne is noted for the Amazon #1 Best Seller, "Called to Be a Soldier". Not only is Wayne an author; but he is certified and mentored by John C. Maxwell, the number one leadership guru in the world. As a steward of leadership and inspiration, Wayne believes that everyone can reach their fullest potential with the proper guidance, motivation and inspiration.

Wayne is the CEO and founder of L. Wayne Smalls & Associates LLC., a leadership training and consulting company that assists individuals and organizations in empowering, enabling and enhancing leaders to grow. He is also the CEO of Leader Lifestylez, Inc. Some of the services that are provided are keynotes, motivational speeches leadership coaching and training, team building workshops, seminars and mastermind groups.

Wayne is the host of his own leadership talk radio show, Leader Lifestylez, which airs on WIDU 99.7 FM every Monday at 9:00 AM. Wayne is a part of several mentoring groups in the community and has a strong passion for helping others to achieve their dreams.

SPECIAL THANKS

I would like to give special thanks to some incredible people that have been of great support to me in my personal growth and development, as well as helping to make this book a huge success:

I would like to thank my wife, **Loyda Smalls**, for supporting me in all of my endeavors. Her expertise in administration, organization, and planning has been invaluable to our company, L. Wayne Smalls & Associates, LLC. where she is also the president of the company. Additonally, she helps me by giving me the time and freedom to express my creativity in something that I am very passionate about, leadership.

I would like to thank my mother, **Joyce Vance**, who has supported me my entire life. Her leadership, guidance, and support has helped me to become the man that I am today. She has always provided me with a great example of what great leadership looks like. She was also very instrumental in the success of this project.

I would like to thank my friend and partner, **Genise Barber**, for supporting me in our various business endeavors. She has proven to be a great friend, partner, visionary, and inspiration in a world where good, genuine people are hard to find. She is also the President of a non-profit organization that we formed together, Leader Lifestylez, Inc.

www.ingramcontent.com/pod-product-compliance
Lightning Source LLC
Chambersburg PA
CBHW071209220526
45468CB00002B/557